I THINK, AND THEN I ACT

.. IT SEEMS TO MAKE MORE SENSE

ASHOK JAHAGIRDAR

Made with ♥ on the Notion Press Platform
www.notionpress.com

THIS BOOK IS DEDICATED TO,

THOSE WHO BELIEVE,

REASON IS PERMANENT,

EMOTIONS ARE TRANSITORY.

Contents

Foreword

In the realm where thoughts take flight,
"I Think, and Then I Act" ignites the light.
A poetic journey of the heart and mind,
A tale of the choices that we each must find.
In words that dance and ideas that sing,
This book's a beacon, a profound offering.
In lyrical verses, it gently unveils,
The power of thoughts, the wind in our sails.
So let us wander through its pages deep,
Where wisdom blooms, like secrets we keep.
This book, a compass in the vast unknown,
Guides us to the path that's all our own.

Preface

Let me mention at the very outset that I never intended this to be a "SELF HELP" book. In fact, far from it. I truly believe that every single person on this planet marches to a different tune, so, personally I cant see how I can make suggestions. Simply because – in the best scenario – only that person knows "the lay of the land".

Look at this as if two friends are meeting over a cup of tea, sharing random experiences they have had and observations they may have made in their own separate lives.

By profession I'm a teacher. Over the past thirty years, I have had the good fortune, to teach a wide spectrum of students ranging from a 3 year old, yes, a 3 year old, whom I taught how to write computer programs, of course they were simple, to a 92 year old who wanted to connect with his grandchildren in the US. From students who wanted to acquire specific programming skills to senior managers who found that they had to learn the basic computer skills to keep pace with their juniors or senior executives from other companies, with whom they would interact during "high level" meetings.

During the course of this it was quite natural I came across individuals with completely different profiles.

For me that was a blessing. During classes, I observed different individuals had their own unique way of learning. Because of this I would say I learnt a lot and realised that teaching should be a "bidirectional" process, sometimes the teacher gives and the student receives, BUT THERE ARE TIMES WHEN THE

STUDENT GIVES - THE TEACHER SHOULD BE READY TO RECEIVE.

CHAPTER ONE

A TALE OF FIRE, A MAN, AND A TIGER

In the face of adversity, human beings have an ability to remain calm and composed, even when confronted with the most difficult of situations. This capacity for level-headedness is beautifully exemplified in a hypothetical scenario: a fire breaks out on a floor in a building, trapping a man and a tiger inside. While instinct would dictate that panic and chaos ensue, the man's decision to calmly retrieve a fire extinguisher and extinguish the flames speaks to the mans ability to triumph over chaos.

The first aspect of this scenario that warrants consideration is the presence of a fire. Fires are notorious for evoking fear and panic in both humans and animals. They unleash an uncontrollable force of destruction, engulfing everything in their path. The flickering flames and the suffocating smoke are enough to incite fear, even in the bravest of souls. Yet, within this menacing context, we find our central character, a man. Here, the man represents the symbol of human rationality and the ability to think clearly amidst pandemonium.

Amidst the chaos of the fire, it is the man's recognition of a fire extinguisher that sets the narrative on its remarkable course. The fire extinguisher is not merely an object; it is a symbol of human ingenuity, a tribute to mans ability to devise solutions in the face of adversity. It signifies the power of preparation and a commitment to safeguard life and property. In this scenario, the fire extinguisher represents the embodiment of human knowledge and technology harnessed to combat the destructive power of fire.

As the man calmly walks to the fire extinguisher, amidst the deafening roar of the flames and the frenzied pacing of the trapped tiger, the man moves with a serenity that only logic can provide. His composure in the face of imminent danger highlights the remarkable quality of human resilience. It is as if the man's actions are guided by an inner wisdom, a deep well of knowledge about fire safety and the means to control the blaze.

Once he reaches the fire extinguisher, the man's actions display an intrinsic understanding of its operation. He is not daunted by the chaotic circumstances surrounding him but approaches his task methodically and efficiently. The extinguisher's discharge of suppressant agent onto the flames represents the man's capacity to confront adversity.

When the man successfully extinguishes the fire, he brings an end to the calamity that threatened his and the tiger's lives. It is in this moment of triumph that we see the true essence of human capability. It showcases our ability to harness knowledge, technology, and our capacity for calm decision-making to surmount even the most daunting challenges.

The man's actions in the face of adversity are symbolic of real-life situations where individuals have displayed extraordinary courage and presence of mind. Whether it be in the midst of natural disasters, accidents, or unforeseen emergencies, humans have repeatedly demonstrated their capacity to remain calm and take decisive action when others might succumb to panic.

In conclusion, the scenario of a fire, a man, and a tiger trapped inside a building encapsulates the remarkable human trait of maintaining composure in the midst of chaos. It underscores our ability to think rationally, employ technology, and, most importantly, take decisive action to avert disaster. This tale serves as a testament to the indomitable human spirit, reminding us that even in the most challenging circumstances, our capacity for calm and reasoned decision-making can ultimately help us triumph over chaos.

CHAPTER TWO

SLOW DOWN, DON'T SPEED UP

Slowing down may seem to you as counterproductive in our fast-paced world, but I have found applying the brakes, once in a while, has made a positive difference in my life.

So often, my smartphone is buzzing with notifications, the emails are piling up, and my to-do list stretches to infinity.

I'm quite sure this a familiar scenario for many of you. In this whirlwind of activity, one would have thought taking a moment to think before is like a luxury one couldn't afford. But here's the paradox – I have observed, that it's precisely in these hectic times that thinking before acting becomes crucial.

We often equate speed with progress. We rush through decisions, believing we're being efficient, but too often, we end up making hasty choices, leading to setbacks and regrets. But I have found taking a pause, no matter how brief, provides me with the clarity and insight I need to make the right decisions.

I have realised – patience is not just a virtue; it's a practical tool in my decision-making toolkit.

There have been times when I have sent an email in the heat of the moment and I wished I could take it back. I wish I had applied the brakes. I wish I had taken a pause.

There have been several occasions when I have acted on impulse, perhaps said something without thinking or made a snap decision.

Whenever Ive sent a fiery email, or made an impromptu purchase, or said something I didn't mean, in the heat of an argument, the consequences of my impulsive actions have been painful.

Ill be truthful enough to admit that my impulsive actions have often led to regrets and unintended consequences.

But why did I act on impulse in the first place?

I realised that "impulsivity" is a natural human trait. Our brains are wired to react quickly to perceived threats or opportunities. It's a survival mechanism. However, in the modern world, this impulse has fairly often led me astray.

In the tumultuous theater of life, our actions often take center stage, illuminated only by the unforgiving spotlight of impulse. We've all been there, making decisions in the heat of the moment, acting on impulse, only to later regret our hasty choices.

I call it "The Impulse Dilemma". I thought to myself "If I had taken a pause, would I have become a slow, indecisive turtle ?"

It's then that I realised that taking a pause would have made me a wiser, more intentional decision-maker. I realised that impulsivity, often synonymous with spontaneity, held for me the allure of the immediate. That's why I was inclined to act swiftly and without forethought.

But, I realised that while impulse can lead to some exhilarating moments, it's often a double-edged sword. That impulsive choices have had a domino effect on my life. They have strained relationships, dented my wallet, and left me with lingering regrets. So, if you've ever felt rushed into choices you later regret, you are definitely not alone.

I observed that my impulsive decisions can be rash, emotional, and, in the end, ill-advised. The key is recognizing when to harness the power of impulse and when to curb its influence.

Its then that I realised the power of the "Pause Button".

I found that the metaphorical "Pause Button" gives me the time to understand the context and gather relevant information, before taking a decision.

Also, then, I could weigh different courses of action, considering both short-term and long-term consequences.

However I had to keep reminding myself that this was not about stifling spontaneity or excitement; it's about striking a balance between quick decisions and thoughtful actions.

The pause button allowed my logical brain to kick in, preventing me from taking irrational decisions.

So, if I had to take a immediate decision, I would take a breath and count to ten before speaking or acting. I found that when I did that, it was as if I was "throwing impulsivity out of the window".

If the decision was not to be taken immediately, I would give myself a "24 hour window" before making a choice.

It was then that I discovered my brain had two systems that came into play whenever I had to take a decision.

My brain's System 1, the fast and automatic decision-making system contributed to my impulsive actions. It was designed for quick responses and could be triggered by emotional reactions. I saw my impulsive actions as a manifestation of System 1 on overdrive, leading me to act without understanding the consequences.

CHAPTER THREE

THE TWO SYSTEMS

System 1, I called "The Fast and Automatic System". It's the one uses when you swerve to avoid an oncoming car or catch a ball without thinking. I also understood that System 1 wasn't tailor made for complex, thoughtful choices.

System 2, I called "The Slow and Analytical System". This system was more deliberate and rational. It helped me to carefully analyse situations, weigh options available to me and consider the consequences of the options.

I realised that System 1 could lead me astray because of cognitive biases taking over. I refer to cognitive biases as a mental shortcuts where I found I was using only data that fitted my preconceptions. I did not look for a confirmation. Also I was using data that was easily and immediately available. (I agree, its human to do so.)

Also I observed that certain decisions I had taken were clouded by my emotions. So my decision was more of a emotional reaction, rather than a intelligent response.

So the next time I had to act, I tried to make sure I was not relying on System 1, where my cognitive biases and emotions would influence my action.

There also have been times when I didn't have the information that I needed to take the right decision on hand. I would then talk to a trusted friend, mentor, or advisor. I found that their inputs helped me get a "complete the picture" , as if the jigsaw puzzle was now complete.

CHAPTER FOUR

ROLE OF EMOTIONS

IN THE ENIGMATIC WORLD OF DECISION MAKING, LOGIC AND EMOTION ENGAGE IN AN ETERNAL TUG OF WAR. IN THIS THEATER OF THE MIND, EMOTIONS OFTEN TAKE CENTER STAGE, AND I MUST SAY, THEY MAKE QUITE THE UNRULY ACTORS.

THE HUMAN BRAIN, A COMPLEX ORGAN TEEMING WITH NEURONS, IS THE PRODUCER OF OUR DAILY DRAMAS. AND LIKE ANY GREAT PRODUCER, IT ADORES AN ENTERTAINING SPECTACLE. ENTER EMOTIONS, THOSE FLAMBOYANT ACTORS, TO SPICE THINGS UP. NO DECISION IS TOO SMALL FOR THEIR DRAMATIC FLAIR. FROM CHOOSING A CEREAL FOR BREAKFAST TO DECIDING

TO QUIT YOUR JOB, EMOTIONS ARE THERE, CHANNELLING THEIR INNER DIVAS.

FIRST ON OUR STAGE IS "FEAR," THE MASTER OF DISASTER. IT ENTERS WITH A GRAND FLOURISH, DROWNING LOGIC IN A SEA OF IRRATIONAL "WHAT-IFS." JUST WHEN YOU'RE ABOUT TO MAKE A SENSIBLE INVESTMENT, FEAR GLEEFULLY INTERRUPTS, "WHAT IF THE ECONOMY CRASHES? WHAT IF YOU END UP BROKE AND HOMELESS?" SUDDENLY, YOU'RE BURYING YOUR LIFE SAVINGS IN THE BACKYARD, CONVINCED YOU'LL SOON BE TRADING ACORNS FOR ESSENTIALS.

THEN THERE'S "HAPPINESS," THE WHIMSICAL SPRITE OFTEN PERSUADES US TO MAKE UNWISE CHOICES. "GO AHEAD, BUY THAT NEW SPORTS CAR!" IT EXCLAIMS, BLISSFULLY UNAWARE OF YOUR IMPENDING BANKRUPTCY. THE SENSE OF EUPHORIA BLINDS YOU TO THE PRACTICALITY OF FINANCING, MAINTENANCE COSTS, AND THE FACT THAT YOU LIVE IN A CITY WHERE PARKING IS CLOSE TO IMPOSSIBLE.

AH, "LOVE," THE MOST ENCHANTING ACTOR OF THEM ALL. IT HAS A KNACK FOR PUSHING US INTO WHIRLWIND ROMANCES, DECLARING, "HE'S THE ONE!" OR "SHE'S YOUR SOULMATE!" ALL OF THIS, OF COURSE, WITHOUT CONSULTING OUR RATIONAL SIDE. "LOVE" THRIVES ON IMPULSIVITY, SENDING US ON ROLLERCOASTER RELATIONSHIPS THAT ARE AS SHORT-LIVED AS A SUMMER FLING.

AND WE MUSTN'T FORGET "ANGER," THE HOT-TEMPERED FIREBRAND WHO CAN TURN EVEN THE MOST SENSIBLE DECISIONS INTO VOLCANIC ERUPTIONS. WHEN A FRUSTRATING CUSTOMER SERVICE CALL GOES AWRY, "ANGER" INSISTS ON REVENGE, DEMANDING YOU WAGE A WAR VIA A SCATHING REVIEW THAT COULD'VE BEEN AVOIDED WITH A COOL HEAD AND A POLITE EMAIL.

NEXT IS "GUILT," THE GUILT-TRIP SPECIALIST. IT INSISTS ON DECISIONS THAT MAKE YOU FEEL LIKE A HUMANITARIAN, NO MATTER HOW IMPRACTICAL. SHOULD YOU DONATE YOUR ENTIRE MONTH'S SALARY TO THE LOCAL ANIMAL SHELTER? ACCORDING TO "GUILT," ABSOLUTELY, EVEN IF IT

MEANS YOU SURVIVE ON INSTANT RAMEN FOR THE REST OF THE MONTH.

LASTLY, THE MEDDLESOME "PEER PRESSURE" IS THE COUSIN OF EMOTION, AND IT OFTEN LEADS TO SOME OF THE MOST BEWILDERING DECISIONS. "EVERYONE'S DOING IT!" IT PROCLAIMS, ENCOURAGING YOU TO BUY THAT TOAST MAKER, JOIN A CULT, OR TRY EXTREME POGO-STICKING, ALL BECAUSE YOUR FRIENDS ARE DOING IT. THE FACT THAT YOU LIVE IN A THIRD FLOOR APARTMENT WITH A LOW CEILING IS IRRELEVANT.

NOW, WHEN THESE CAPRICIOUS ACTORS GATHER FOR A GRAND FINALE, IT'S LIKE A CHAOTIC OPERA OF CHAOS. PICTURE THIS: YOU'RE OFFERED A JOB IN A NEW CITY, AND YOUR EMOTIONS LINE UP LIKE DIVAS IN A CAST CALL. FEAR SCREAMS, "YOU'LL BE ALONE AND MISERABLE!" LOVE PLEADS, "BUT YOUR CRUSH LIVES THERE!" HAPPINESS INSISTS, "THINK OF THE ADVENTURE!" MEANWHILE, LOGIC, THE UNDERAPPRECIATED UNDERSTUDY, IS WAITING IN THE WINGS, BARELY HEARD.

YES, EMOTIONS DO INDEED PLAY A VITAL ROLE IN DECISION MAKING. THEY ADD COLOUR AND UNPREDICTABILITY TO LIFE'S DULL SCRIPT, MAKING SURE WE NEVER HAVE A BORING MOMENT. THEY GUIDE US, CHALLENGE US, AND SOMETIMES LEAD US DOWN RABBIT HOLES WE NEVER ANTICIPATED. BUT LET'S NOT FORGET THE DIRECTOR – OUR RATIONAL MIND, THE ONE THAT, WHEN GIVEN A MOMENT TO SHINE, CAN MAKE THOSE DECISIONS WITH A TOUCH OF WISDOM.

SO, WHEN THE EMOTIONS START A MELODRAMATIC CHORUS, REMEMBER TO GIVE LOGIC ITS WELL-DESERVED CHANCE TO STEP INTO THE LIMELIGHT. AFTER ALL, IT'S THE CALM AND COLLECTED STAR THAT CAN BRING SOME ORDER TO THIS UPROARIOUS ENSEMBLE. IN THE GRAND PRODUCTION OF LIFE'S DECISION MAKING, LET US EMBRACE THE QUIRKY CAST, BUT ENSURE THE DIRECTOR GETS ITS SAY – FOR, IN THE END, A PINCH OF REASON CAN MAKE EVEN THE MOST FLAMBOYANT SHOW A HIT.

You will say "Aren't our emotions the vibrant hues that paint our experiences, infusing our lives with meaning and depth - that are the driving force behind our decisions, leading us towards joy, love, and fulfilment?" I couldn't agree less. But they can also be the source of impulsive actions, regrets, and turmoil. I realised that the ability to control and manage your emotions is crucial in making rational decisions. Yes, I know emotions can provide valuable information, but they have to be held in check to avoid impulsive actions.

I also fully agree that emotions play a positive role in my decision-making. I call it "The Emotive Symphony".

Theres a fancy term for it "Emotional Intelligence" or "Emotional Quotient".

To me it simply means recognizing, understanding, and managing my emotions. I observed if I could do that, I could navigate the turbulent seas of my emotions and I could make choices that were both rational and compassionate. I realised that just as my emotions could be a valuable source of information, they could also cloud my judgment. I wondered "How could I balance my emotional responses with rational thinking to make more effective decisions?"

I realised that in the intricate landscape of decision-making, emotions can also act as the wind beneath our wings.

I realised the role played by "emotional intelligence". But I also knew that I had to harness my feelings in such a manner so that my decisions aligned with my goals.

I realised that if I could recognise and understanding my emotions it would be my first step towards better decision-making.

I observed that when I became aware of my feelings, I could can prevent them from clouding my judgment.

CHAPTER FIVE

MINDFULNESS AND STRATEGIC THINKING

To me mindfulness means simply staying in the present moment.

We live in an age of constant distraction. The pings and notifications from our devices demand our attention, make it extremely challenging to focus on the present moment. I found that this constant multitasking was hindering my ability to "THINK, AND THEN ACT".

decisions that were driven solely by fleeting emotions.

I observed that if I was not judgmental about my thoughts and feelings, it became easier for me to "stay in the present moment." Because if I stayed in the present moment, my focus improved and it became easier for me to shift from System 1 or "The Fast and Automatic System" to System 2, or "The Slow and Analytical System". Also by "staying in the moment", my thoughts became much clearer than before. In other words when I removed the mental clutter, I was able to analyze the situation and consider the options available to me. I

I have found that when I clear the mental clutter, it becomes far easier for me to analyze the situation and consider the options available tom me.

In the intricate web of life's decision-making, strategic thinking emerges as a guiding star, illuminating the path to thoughtful and purposeful choices. Many of you may think that when I use the term "strategic thinking", Im sitting a war room, planning my next move to take the enemy off – guard. Sorry to disappoint you. Its not all exciting - strategic thinking is far from a cryptic process shrouded in mystery.

I simply try to take a long term view and then check if the decision that I will take, not only aligns with my immediate desires but also resonates with my goals.

So I would look at a plethora of alternatives before arriving at a choice. This is an intentional and deliberate approach, so compared to any other approach, this approach is more likely to succeed.

I also look out for the risks lurking in the shadows of my decision. What might go awry, and how likely is it to show up ? I have realised the importance of not discounting the possible pitfalls that are linked to my decision.

Im also aware that any significant decision requires resources for execution. Whether it's time, money, or other assets. I a note of what I consider I need and whether I have those resources or I will be required to procure them.

When I ask my friends or mentors to provide feedback on decisions I would be taking, that feedback has helped me to filter out

unnecessary that have crept into my decision.

CHAPTER SIX

THE SWOT ANALYSIS

Within the toolkit of strategic thinking, I looked at SWOT analysis stands as a useful tool:

Strengths: I began by identifying my strengths, both as an individual and specifically related to the decision I had to take. What were the advantage I had? What were the assets that I possessed?

Weaknesses: What were my weaknesses? How could I overcome them?

Opportunities: What were the opportunities that would be a "fall out" of my chosen course of action. Were there any other possibilities on the horizon?

Threats: I tried to identify any potential threats or obstacles that may stand in my path. If I was able to identify them, I could try and navigate around them.

WE OFTEN FIND OURSELVES STUMBLING OVER THE SAME AGE-OLD HURDLES. THESE BARRIERS, KNOWN AS "OBSTACLES," SEEM TO POSSESS A PECULIAR TALENT FOR LEAPING RIGHT INTO OUR PATH WHEN WE LEAST EXPECT IT.

THE TROUBLE WITH OBSTACLES IS THAT THEY DON'T COME WITH GPS COORDINATES OR NEON SIGNS. INSTEAD, THEY'RE STEALTHY LITTLE NINJAS, LURKING IN THE SHADOWS OF EVERYDAY LIFE. YOU MAY THINK YOU'RE ABOUT TO ACE THAT JOB INTERVIEW, BUT OH NO, HERE COMES AN OBSTACLE DISGUISED AS A POP QUIZ ON QUANTUM PHYSICS! BEFORE YOU PANIC, REMEMBER: THINKING IS YOUR TRUSTY NINJA WEAPON.

LET'S FACE IT; EMOTIONS AND OBSTACLES ARE LIKE PEANUT BUTTER AND JELLY - A CLASSIC COMBINATION, BUT NOT ALWAYS THE MOST PRACTICAL. WHEN YOU RELY ON FEELINGS TO GUIDE YOU, YOU MIGHT FIND YOURSELF WANDERING OFF INTO THE MAZE OF DESPAIR. THIS IS WHERE THINKING COMES TO THE RESCUE, BRANDISHING ITS LOGICAL SWORD.

SUPPOSE, YOU'RE STUCK IN AN ELEVATOR WITH A PERSISTENT OBSTACLE - CLAUSTROPHOBIA. YOU COULD ALLOW YOUR EMOTIONS TO "TAKE THE WHEEL" AND AT ONCE PANIC WOULD SET IN, LIKE A UNWANTED GUEST AT A PARTY. OR YOU COULD ENGAGE YOUR THINKING NINJA TO REMIND YOU THAT ELEVATORS ARE STATISTICALLY SAFER THAN, SAY, WANDERING INTO A BEAR'S DEN. SUDDENLY, THAT TINY SPACE BECOMES MORE OF A COZY CLOSET THAN A TORTURE CHAMBER.

NOW, I MUST ADMIT, OBSTACLES CAN BE RATHER AMUSING. THEY HAVE A KNACK FOR MAKING US QUESTION THE VERY FABRIC OF OUR EXISTENCE. TAKE, FOR EXAMPLE, THE HUMBLE "TANGLED

HEADPHONES" OBSTACLE. IT'S A SIMPLE TASK: UNTANGLE THOSE WIRES, AND VOILÀ, MUSIC TO YOUR EARS. BUT THE WIRES HAVE OTHER PLANS. THEY TWIST AND TURN, DEFY LOGIC, AND SOMEHOW MANAGE TO IMPERSONATE SPAGHETTI IN A QUANTUM PHYSICS EXPERIMENT. HERE, THINKING CAN COME TO THE RESCUE AS YOU METHODICALLY ANALYZE THE KNOTS, GENTLY REMINDING YOURSELF THAT LIFE IS TOO SHORT TO WRESTLE WITH INANIMATE OBJECTS. A FEW STRATEGIC MOVEMENTS, AND YOU'RE BACK TO YOUR FAVORITE TUNES.

NOW, SPEAKING OF NOODLES, LET'S DIVE INTO THE CULINARY ARENA. THE "DINNER PARTY DISASTER" OBSTACLE OFTEN LURKS, WAITING TO POUNCE ON OUR CULINARY ASPIRATIONS. YOU PLANNED AN ELEGANT SOIRÉE WITH A GOURMET MENU, BUT IN WALKS MR. OBSTACLE, IN THE FORM OF A BURNT LASAGNA. FEELINGS OF DESPAIR THREATEN TO TAKE OVER, BUT THINKING SWOOPS IN, SAVING THE DAY WITH A BACKUP PLAN: PIZZA DELIVERY. YOU MAY NOT HAVE IMPRESSED YOUR GUESTS WITH YOUR CULINARY PROWESS, BUT YOU'VE GIVEN THEM A MEMORABLE TALE OF YOUR CULINARY

MISADVENTURES.

OBSTACLES ALSO HAVE A KNACK FOR MAKING US QUESTION OUR SANITY. TAKE THE "LOST CAR KEYS" OBSTACLE, FOR EXAMPLE. YOU'RE READY TO EMBARK ON A GRAND ADVENTURE WHEN THOSE LITTLE METALLIC DEVILS VANISH INTO THIN AIR. EMOTIONS THREATEN TO TURN YOU INTO A HUMAN TORNADO, BUT THINKING STEPS IN AND SAYS, "HEY, REMEMBER THE HOOK BY THE DOOR WHERE YOU WERE SUPPOSED TO HANG THOSE KEYS? LET'S TRY THERE!" LO AND BEHOLD, YOUR NINJA THINKING HAS GUIDED YOU TO SUCCESS, AND THE CAR KEYS ARE FOUND. OBSTACLE OVERCOME!

OBSTACLES CAN BE AN ENTERTAINING CIRCUS ACT IN THE THREE-RING CIRCUS OF LIFE. THEY PRANCE AROUND, PERFORMING THEIR TRICKS, AND INVITE US TO JOIN THE FUN.

While emotions might send us on a rollercoaster ride of frustration, thinking allows us to navigate these hurdles with style and grace.

So, next time an obstacle leaps in your way, remember that thinking is your trusty ninja warrior, who is here to vanquish the challenges that life throws at you. Embrace the humour in the absurdity of these roadblocks, and you'll find that with a clear mind and a sense of humour, no obstacle is too daunting, no situation too dire, and no tangle of wires too complicated to untangle.

So, let us embrace THINKING, this superpower, become more present in our choices, a think before we act, so that we act with greater clarity and awareness.

In the face of the impulse dilemma, our salvation lies in thinking before we act. It's about embracing that metaphorical pause button we explored in Chapter 2. If I had taken a moment to consider the consequences of my actions it would have helped me us avoid needless headaches and would also have ensured that my choices align were aligned with my long-term goals.

CHAPTER SEVEN

STRATEGIC THINKING

When I refer to the term "strategic thinking", you must be wondering whether I am in a war room, planning my next move, to outfox the enemy. Im sorry to disappoint you, its far less exciting

On the other hand it is not also a pedantic overcomplication of decisions. Rather, it is a balanced and methodical approach, designed to enhance the probability of successful outcomes. In the forthcoming chapters, we will explore methods to avoid analysis paralysis and embrace diverse.

When I have to take a significant decision I try to define a set of criteria to evaluate my options. This creates a structured approach to decision-making and reduces the chances my getting lost in a sea of data.

While it's essential to gather information and analyze it, don't ignore your gut feeling. Sometimes, your intuition provides valuable insights that data can't convey.

Whenever I find yourself unable to make a decision, I don't hesitate to seek advice from a trusted friend or mentor. A different perspective often helps me break the cycle of overthinking.

Sometimes I find myself revisiting a decision. I try to break that cycle by asking myself what is the worst possible outcome can provide clarity. Recognizing that the worst-case scenario is often not as dire as our imagination can calm your fears.

Also I keep reminding myself that no decision is ever perfect. There will always be an element of uncertainty and risk. Rather than striving for the impossible ideal of a flawless decision, I aim for decisions that are well-informed, that are aligned with your values, and can be made within a reasonable time frame.

CHAPTER EIGHT

THE POWER OF DIVERSE PERSPECTIVES

Our individual perspectives are like the facets of a precious gem, each offering a unique angle on a situation. When we seek out diverse viewpoints, we gain access to a broader spectrum of experiences, wisdom, and insights. This, in turn, helps us to make more well-rounded decisions.

When you take a decision making, your perspective is a brushstroke of unique colours, but a complete painting often requires the blending of multiple viewpoints.

So I don't hesitate to seek out different perspectives. I ask for advice, and I collaborate with others, knowing that this will enrich my choices and expand my horizons

Mentally I have created a personal board of advisors consisting of individuals with diverse backgrounds, experiences, and expertise. Whenever I have to take an important decisions I consult with them.

I also have a "Devil's Advocate" ready. That person challenges my viewpoints and my decision-making rationale. I have found this helps me uncover potential weaknesses in my choices.

Whenever I am required to take a complex decisions, I always involve a group of people. I know that collaborative decision-making leverages the collective intelligence.

I have realised that if I have to truly embrace diverse perspectives, I have to let go of my ego.

I have to be willing to admit that I don't have all the answers and that others may have valuable insights to offer. That humility and openness will help me in my decision-making process.

CHAPTER NINE

NAVIGATING ETHICAL DILEMMAS

In a rapidly changing world, we frequently encounter complex moral choices and ethical dilemmas.

While taking a significant decision, I bring to make sure that my decision will not have any unethical fall out.

I realise, that in a world filled with complex moral choices, ethical decision-making is not a luxury but a necessity. By understanding the importance of ethics, clarifying values and principles, and following a structured approach to ethical decision-making,

individuals and organizations can navigate the most challenging dilemmas while upholding their integrity and contributing to a more ethical world.

I try to make sure that I decide on the most ethical course of action.

CHAPTER TEN

BOUNCING BACK FROM FAILURE

I know that sometimes, things won't go as planned. That I should learn from my setbacks and come back even stronger.

After all, in the tapestry of life, setbacks and failures are the threads that weave resilience.

I have found that setbacks and failures are an inevitable part of our journey. The road to success is often paved with failures. However, it is not the failures themselves but our response to them that defines our path forward. Resilience is the key to overcoming obstacles and using them as stepping stones.

I have realised that each setback is a lesson in disguise. It offers me an opportunity to reflect on what went wrong, what could have been done differently, and how I could avoid similar pitfalls in the future.

I know that resilience is not just about bouncing back but also about adapting to new circumstances. I have to be open to altering my approach and I and accepting that not all plans will work.

I know that failure can be emotionally taxing. At such times I always take the support of my friends and family.

I try not to look at success as a linear path. I know it often involves setbacks and detours. I know I have to redefine my notion of success to encompass the journey, not just the destination.

Resilience is closely linked to perseverance. It's the commitment to keep moving forward, no matter how many times I have stumbled I have found that perseverance is the engine that propels me through failures toward success.

The path to becoming a better decision-maker is not a final destination but a lifelong journey. The skills and insights I have gained are tools to help me navigate life's twists and turns with greater wisdom and clarity.

I keep reminding myself that resilience is not the absence of failure, but the ability to rise above it. It's about transforming setbacks into stepping stones, learning from every experience, and, ultimately, becoming a stronger and wiser decision-maker.

CHAPTER ELEVEN

CONCLUSION

As we wrap up this "voyage" through the pages of "I Think, Then I Act," – for me, it's been a journey of self-discovery, an odyssey through the vast landscapes of human cognition, and an exploration of how our thoughts sculpt the path of our lives.

Ive ventured into the labyrinth of human decision-making, seeking to understand the intricate dance between our thoughts and our actions.

Like you, I too have grappled with big questions and everyday dilemmas, and I have learnt that the way we think not only shapes our choices but also our very existence.

I have realised that our thoughts are not mere spectators in the grand theater of life. They're the writers, directors, and lead actors. Every choice we make, every step we take, begins with a thought. It's in this understanding that we find the essence of mindful decision-making, a power that can guide us towards a life that's truly our own.

We've started by acknowledging the tremendous power of self-awareness.

CHAPTER TWELVE

CHAPTER THIRTEEN

Epilogue: "I Think, Then I Act" - Navigating Life's Journey

Well, as you and I wrap up this enlightening voyage through the pages of "I Think, Then I Act," it's time for us sit back and reflect on the wisdom we've unearthed together. It's been a journey of self-discovery, an odyssey through the vast landscapes of human cognition, and an exploration of how our thoughts sculpt the path of our lives.

Throughout this book, the both of us have ventured into the labyrinth of human decision-making, seeking to understand the intricate dance between our thoughts and our actions. We've grappled with big questions and everyday dilemmas, learning that the way we think not only shapes our choices but also our very existence.

At the heart of our journey has been the profound realization that our thoughts are not mere spectators in the grand theater of life. They're the writers, directors, and lead actors. Every choice we make, every step we take, begins with a thought. It's in this understanding that we find the essence of mindful decision-making, a power that can guide us towards a life that's truly our own.

We acknowledged the tremendous power of self-awareness. It's a formidable force, allowing us to dig deep into the hidden chambers of our minds and unearth our true desires and values. Armed with this self-awareness, you and I can embark on our life's journey with clarity, choosing pathways that resonate with our core beliefs, aspirations, and identities. We should always remember knowing ourselves is the compass that can keep us from straying too far off course.

Our journey has brought us face to face with the quirks of human cognition. We've taken a close look at cognitive biases, those sneaky mental shortcuts that can sometimes lead us astray. By recognizing these biases, we can outmanoeuvre them, making decisions with a keener eye and a more open mind.

Together, you and I, have also explored the realm of emotional intelligence, a treasure chest of skills that equips us to navigate the rollercoaster of human emotions and relationships. We have seen that theres a difference between reacting impulsively to a provocation and responding thoughtfully with empathy. By tuning into the emotional frequencies of those around us and ourselves, we can harness a powerful tool for harmonious interactions and meaningful decision-making.

We've explored the importance of not just doing what's expedient, but what's right. In a world where shortcuts and moral grey areas can be tempting, we have to remind ourselves that a life lived in harmony with our core values lead us to a profound sense of fulfilment and genuine success.

We have come face to face with the quirks of human cognition. We've taken a close look at cognitive biases, those sneaky mental shortcuts that can sometimes lead us astray. By recognizing these biases, we can outmanoeuvre them, making decisions with a keener eye and a more open mind.

Let's not forget that mindfulness is our faithful companion. Mindfulness provides us with the solid ground on which to build our decisions. Mindfulness is the tool that helps us to become keen observers of our thoughts, and master the skill of staying present and aware. With mindfulness, we can transform mindless reactions into thoughtful responses.

As our journey comes to a close, I want to acknowledge the countless stories of individuals who've harnessed the power of mindful decision-making.

We've heard of leaders who've steered organizations towards success and everyday heroes who've selflessly served their communities, and met ordinary individuals who've harnessed their inner strength to surmount seemingly insurmountable challenges.

These narratives reinforce a fundamental truth: that our lives are a series of choices, and those choices are the stepping stones to our destinies. With every conscious decision, we lay the bricks of our unique life path, etching our story onto the grand canvas of existence.

Let us remember that the art of mindful decision-making is not just a luxury; it's a lifeline. It's a return to the roots of our humanity, an embrace of the profound capability of human thought.

The Greek philosopher Socrates once declared that "an unexamined life is not worth living." I, too, urge you to be the architect of your lives, not just a spectator.

We know that we are not bound by our past choices - we are empowered by the choices we make today. We can choose a path of greater fulfilment, deeper connection, and truer authenticity.

But that's not all. Our journey has also explored the realm of emotional intelligence, a treasure chest of skills that equips us to navigate the rollercoaster of human emotions and relationships. It's the difference between reacting impulsively to a provocation and responding thoughtfully with empathy. By tuning into the emotional frequencies of those around us and ourselves, we harness a powerful tool for harmonious interactions and meaningful decision-making.

We've also delved into the terrain of ethical decision-making. We've explored the importance of not just doing what's expedient, but what's right. In a world where shortcuts and moral grey areas can be tempting, we have book remind ourselves that a life lived in harmony with our core values leads to a profound sense of fulfilment and genuine success.

In the end, the philosophy of "I Think, Then I Act" inspires you and me to live our lives that are masterpieces of intention, painted with strokes of mindfulness, ethical wisdom, and personal truth. So, let us be the artists of our own stories, the architects of our own destinies.

Remember, knowing ourselves is the compass that can keep us from straying too far off course

Let's not forget the art of mindfulness and contemplation, our faithful companions on this journey. These practices provide us with the solid ground on which to build our decisions. They are the tools that enable us to become keen observers of our thoughts, mastering the skill of staying present and aware. With mindfulness, we can transform mindless reactions into thoughtful responses.

As our journey comes to a close, I want to acknowledge the countless stories of individuals who've harnessed the power of mindful decision-making. These stories aren't just tales; they are blueprints for how we can apply the wisdom of this book to our own lives. We've met leaders who've steered organizations towards success, everyday heroes who've selflessly served their communities, and ordinary individuals who've harnessed their inner strength to surmount seemingly insurmountable challenges.

These narratives reinforce a fundamental truth: that our lives are a series of choices, and those choices are the stepping stones to our destinies. With every conscious decision, we lay the bricks of our unique life path, etching our story onto the grand canvas of existence.

As we turn the final page, let's carry the lessons of this book with us. In our rapidly changing world, where distractions are rife, and the pace of life seems to accelerate with each passing day, the art of mindful decision-making is not just a luxury; it's a lifeline. It's a return to the roots of our humanity, an embrace of the profound capability of human thought.

The Greek philosopher Socrates once declared that "an unexamined life is not worth living." This book reiterates that sentiment, urging us to be the architects of our lives, not just spectators. The exploration, the contemplation, and the application of these principles are ongoing, lifelong endeavours, marked by patience, resilience, and a commitment to self-discovery.

It's also a journey filled with the promise of change. For we are not bound by our past choices; we are empowered by the choices we make today. We can choose a path of greater fulfilment, deeper connection, and truer authenticity.

In the end, the philosophy of "I Think, Then I Act" inspires us to live lives that are masterpieces of intention, painted with strokes of mindfulness, ethical wisdom, and personal truth. So, let's be the artists of our own stories, the architects of our own destinies, and the thinkers who shape the world within and around us. In each thoughtful action we take, we craft a narrative that's rich with purpose, meaning, and authenticity.

With that, Ill take your leave ,and encourage you to embark on your own journey of mindful decision-making, making each choice an expression of your unique, authentic self.

www.ingramcontent.com/pod-product-compliance
Lightning Source LLC
LaVergne TN
LVHW021145160826
845679LV00023B/2049

* 9 7 9 8 8 9 1 8 6 0 3 1 5 *